THE SPRING BOOK

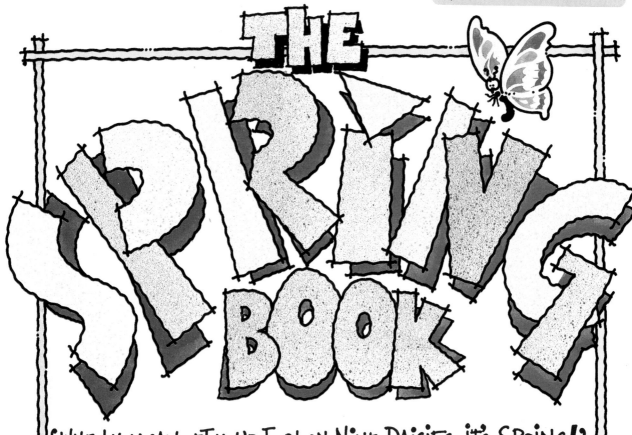

'WHEN YOU CAN SET YOUR FOOT ON NINE DAISIES, IT'S SPRING!'

compiled by Troy Alexander
illustrated by David Farris

Hippo Books
Scholastic Publications Limited
London

Scholastic Publications Ltd.,
10 Earlham Street, London WC2H 9RX, UK

Scholastic Inc.,
730 Broadway, New York, NY 10003, USA

Scholastic Tab Publications Ltd.,
123 Newkirk Road, Richmond Hill,
Ontario L4C 3G5, Canada

Ashton Scholastic Pty. Ltd.,
P O Box 579, Gosford, New South Wales,
Australia

Ashton Scholastic Ltd.,
165 Marua Road, Panmure, Auckland 6,
New Zealand

First published by Scholastic Publications Limited, 1988
This collection copyright © Scholastic Publications Limited, 1988
Illustrations copyright © David Farris, 1988

The publishers and compiler would like to thank the following for their kind permission to include the following copyright material in
this book:
Clean Sheets by Joan Aiken, copyright © Joan Aiken 1973 and reproduced by her kind permission; *The Prayer of the Little Ducks* by
Carmen Bernos de Gasztold and translated by Rumer Godden, copyright © Carmen Bernos de Gasztold and Rumer Godden and
reproduced by kind permission of Macmillan Publishers, London and Basingstoke; *A March Calf* by Ted Hughes, copyright © Ted
Hughes and reproduced by kind permission of Faber and Faber Ltd., from SEASON SONGS by Ted Hughes; *The People Upstairs* by
Ogden Nash, copyright © Ogden Nash 1949, taken from I WOULDN'T HAVE MISSED IT, and reproduced by kind permission of
André Deutsch; *The Blackbird by Belfast Lough* translated by Frank O'Connor, translation copyright © Frank O'Connor and
reproduced by kind permission of A D Peters and Co. Ltd.; *Mary Had a Little Problem* by Emil Pacholek © Emil Pacholek 1987; *The
Kettle Rhyme* by Ian Serraillier, copyright © Ian Serraillier 1950 and reproduced by his kind permission from THE MONSTER HORSE
published by Oxford University Press; *How to Hatch Your Own Egg* adapted from *Egg-shaped Problems* by Anne Woodman,
copyright © Anne Woodman and reproduced by her kind permission from JUNIOR EDUCATION April 1987.

ISBN 0 590 70913 5

We recommend only the use of the following glues: UHU Stick, Pritt Stick, Scotch Pen, paste and children's glue, Stephen's Trufix
paste, Copydex Childsplay, Gloy children's glue.

CONTENTS

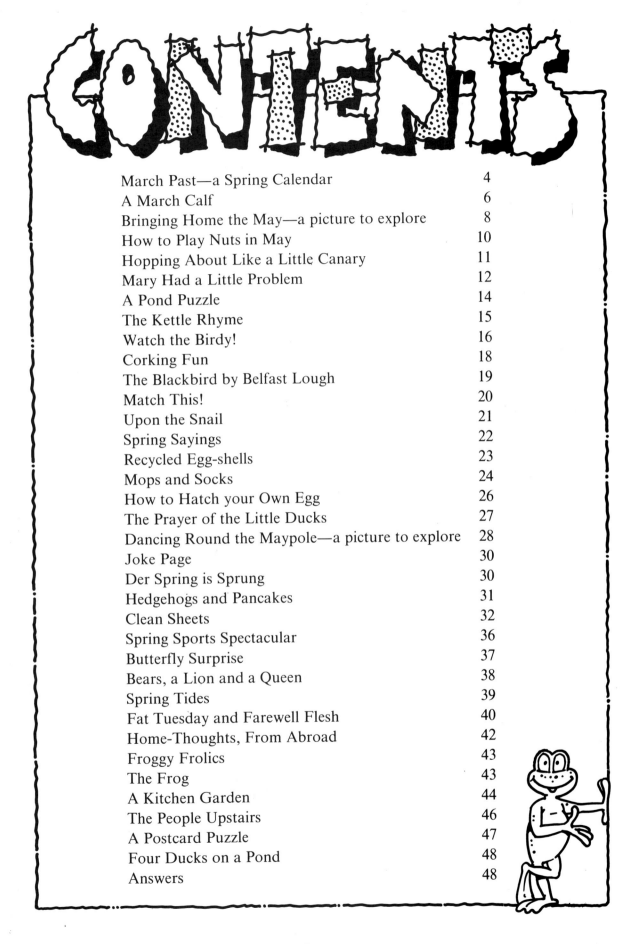

MARCH PAST
A SPRING CALENDAR

1st March: St David's Day. Welsh people may wear a leek or a daffodil—legend says that St David told a Welsh army to wear leeks in their caps so that they could distinguish each other from the Saxons they were about to fight.

17th March: St Patrick's Day. It's said that when St Patrick was preaching in Ireland, he tried to explain the Trinity to the chiefs and priests by showing them the shamrock—three leaves in one. People from Ireland wear shamrocks to commemorate this.

21st March: The vernal equinox, when the day and the night are of equal length. The official start of Spring!

1st April: All Fools' Day. Before midday you can try and fool your friends—and they can try and fool you! Try getting them to look for hen's teeth or peacock's eggs—or give them a tin of tartan paint. In France it's *un poisson d'Avril* (an April fish).

23rd April: St George's Day—and Shakespeare's birthday. If you're English, you can wear a red rose in your buttonhole.

1st May: Mayday! Celebrations up and down the country—look out for the choristers of Magdalen College, Oxford, singing hymns at 6 o'clock in the morning, high up on the top of Magdalen tower, and in Cornwall, the Padstow Oss—actually two Osses, the Old Oss and the Blue Ribbon Oss. They are very splendid hobby horses which dance through the town, accompanied by musicians, and by many townspeople, all wearing decorated hats, ribbons and sashes in the colours of their favourite Oss.

8th May: Helston Furry Dance. In this Cornish town, all the inhabitants wear sprigs of lily of the valley, and many take part in four processional dances through the houses and streets.

The children's dance is at 10 a.m. It gets bigger each year as more and more children join in!

29th May: Oak Apple Day—commemorates King Charles II's escape, by hiding in an oak tree near Boscobel, after he had lost the Battle of Worcester.

At Great Wishford in Wiltshire villagers exercise their right to collect dead wood in Grovely Wood by going early in the morning to pick oak branches. Then four women, carrying small oak branches, dance in Salisbury Cathedral. Afterwards, they stand before the altar with their friends and shout "Grovely! Grovely! Grovely! And all Grovely!"

ALSO DURING SPRING (but on different dates each year)
Shrove Tuesday—the day before the Church's six-week Lenten fast begins has always been a time for special celebrations and events.

At Olney in Buckinghamshire there's a famous Pancake Race. Some say it started in 1445! Today, only women can enter, and they run 425 yards (that's 388 metres) from the Old Bull in the centre of the village to the church, where there is a special service.

The Pancake Race is now international. Since 1950, a Pancake Race has been held in the town of Liberal, in Kansas, USA. The women of Liberal race the women of Olney, and their times are compared to see which town has won each year.

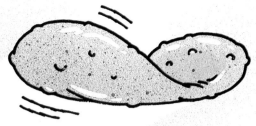

The Scarborough Skipping. Some years ago it was still possible for the people of Scarborough to skip in groups over the heavy ropes swung for them by the fishermen, but the fishing industry has declined, and the road once used has become a dual carriageway! Now smaller groups meet on Southsands Promenade, and skip with ordinary ropes. Some groups go on for three or four hours.

Ascensiontide:
In 1159, during the reign of Henry II, three noblemen out hunting attacked a monk who sheltered a wounded boar. For their punishment, they were ordered to build a hedge of saplings on the sands at low water. Their heirs had to carry on the tradition—or they would lose their lands. Even today, a local farmer and his family still build the Penny Hedge at Whitby in Yorkshire, to make sure of their land!

Many villages in Derbyshire still dress their wells in spring—perhaps once a thanksgiving for clean water that did not run out even in the severest drought! At Tissington, five wells are dressed on Ascension Day. Large boards are covered with clay, and pictures, patterns and texts are made using flower petals, leaves, bark, and other natural materials. The results are spectacularly beautiful.

20th June—the official end of Spring.

A MARCH CALF

by Ted Hughes

Right from the start he is dressed in his best—his
  blacks and his whites.
Little Fauntleroy—quiffed and glossy,
A Sunday suit, a wedding natty get-up,
Standing in dunged straw

Under cobwebby beams, near the mud wall,
Half of him legs,
Shining-eyed, requiring nothing more
But that mother's milk come back often.

Everything else is in order, just as it is.
Let the summer skies hold off, for the moment.
This is just as he wants it.
A little at a time, of each new thing, is best.

Too much and too sudden is too frightening—
When I block the light, a bulk from space,
To let him in to his mother for a suck,
He bolts a yard or two, then freezes,

Staring from every hair in all directions,
Ready for the worst, shut up in his hopeful religion,
A little syllogism
With a wet blue-reddish muzzle, for God's thumb.

You see all his hopes bustling
As he reaches between the worn rails towards
The topheavy oven of his mother.
He trembles to grow, stretching his curl-tip tongue—

What did cattle ever find here
To make this dear little fellow
So eager to prepare himself?
He is already in the race, and quivering to win—

His new purpled eyeball swivel-jerks
In the elbowing push of his plans.
Hungry people are getting hungrier,
Butchers developing expertise and markets,

But he just wobbles his tail—and glistens
Within his dapper profile
Unaware of how his whole lineage
Has been tied up.

He shivers for feel of the world licking his side.
He is like an ember—one glow
Of lighting himself up
With the fuel of himself, breathing and brightening.

Soon he'll plunge out, to scatter his seething joy,
To be present at the grass,
To be free on the surface of such a wideness,
To find himself himself. To stand. To moo.

BRINGING HOME

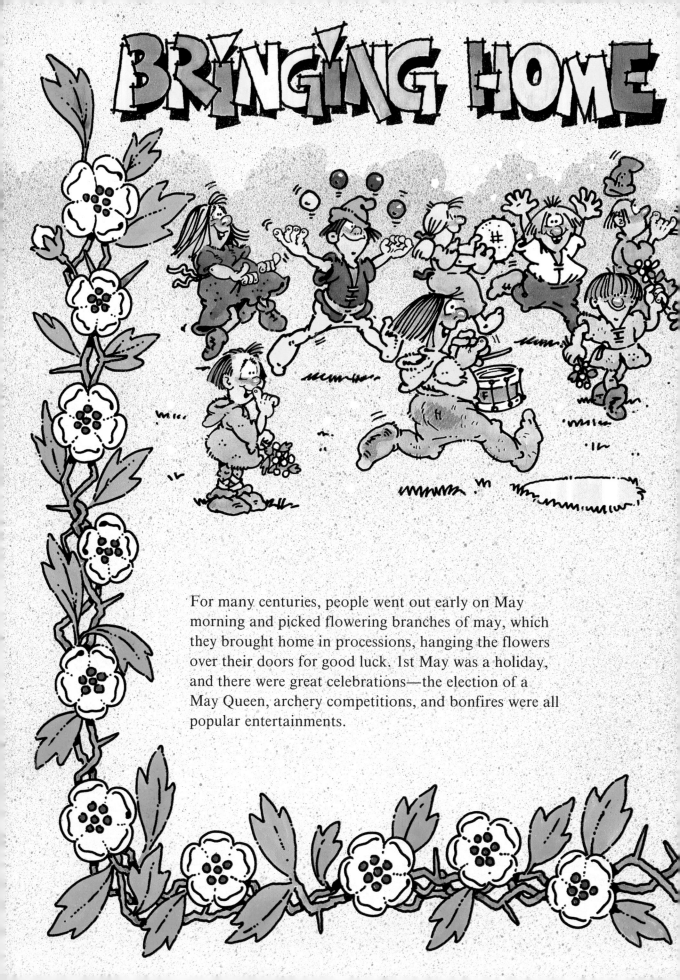

For many centuries, people went out early on May morning and picked flowering branches of may, which they brought home in processions, hanging the flowers over their doors for good luck. 1st May was a holiday, and there were great celebrations—the election of a May Queen, archery competitions, and bonfires were all popular entertainments.

HOW TO PLAY

HERE WE GO GATHERING NUTS IN MAY NUTS IN MAY, NUTS IN MAY

Who will you have for nuts in May,
Nuts in May, nuts in May?
Who will you have for nuts in May
On a cold and frosty morning?

We'll have———for nuts in May,
Nuts in May, nuts in May.
We'll have———for nuts in May
On a cold and frosty morning.

Who will you send to fetch him/her away,
To fetch him/her away, to fetch him/her away?
Who will you send to fetch him/her away
On a cold and frosty morning?

We'll send———to fetch him/her away,
To fetch him/her away, to fetch him/her away.
We'll send———to fetch him/her away
On a cold and frosty morning.

You need two teams of equal size to play this old game! The teams should form straight lines, facing each other, but with space to walk forward and back.

In the middle of the two lines place a handkerchief on the ground. The first team sings the first verse, and as the line walks forward, up to the hanky, the second team walks back. Try to keep the same distance between the two lines that you started with!

The second team sings the second verse. The first team sings the third verse calling out the name of someone in the second team in the space. The second team sings the fourth verse. The first team sings the fifth verse, naming someone in their own team in the space.

At the end of the verses, the two people who have been named come forward, take each other's right hands, and try to pull each other over the hanky. Take care not to pull too hard and hurt someone! Whoever gets pulled over is "captured", and joins the other team. Now reverse the order, so that the second team becomes the first. This can go on until everyone has had a turn, or until there's nobody left in one team!

Nuts in May are really "knots of may"—bunches of flowering hawthorn.

NUTS IN MAY

HERE WE GO GATHERING NUTS IN MAY, ON A COLD AND FROSTY MORNING

HOPPING ABOUT LIKE A LITTLE CANARY

Most people have played catch, hide-and-seek, or blind man's buff, but there are many other games as old as these that it might be fun to dust off and try this Spring!

BLIND BELL

All players are blindfolded, except one, who has a bell. He rings the bell, and all the others try to catch him. When he is caught, he changes places with his catcher.

THE GAME OF CONTRARY

Here I go round the rules of contrary
Hopping about like a little canary
When I say "hold fast", leave go,
When I say "leave go", hold fast.

Form a ring. Each player holds the ends of a handkerchief or scarf. One person is in the centre, and acts as leader. The ring circles slowly, and the leader says the words of the rhyme. Suddenly he calls out one of the commands. If he says "hold fast", all the players must drop their handkerchiefs, and when he shouts "leave go", they all hold on. Forfeits must be paid for mistakes, and you can finish the game when everyone has paid a forfeit.

FIRE, AIR AND WATER

All the players sit in a circle. One player has a ball on a string. He throws it at another player at random, holding on to the end of the piece of string, and calls out "air", "fire", or "water". Before the end of a count of ten, the player who has caught the ball must name an inhabitant of the given element. When FIRE is called, there must be complete silence. For any mistakes, a forfeit must be paid. If you pay three forfeits, you're out!

MARY HAD A LITTLE PROBLEM

by EMIL PACHOLEK

"SORRY I'M LATE, MISS," said my best friend Mary as she came into the classroom looking all hot and bothered.

Miss Frost looked over the top of her spectacles and sighed.

"Well? And what is your excuse, young lady?" she asked wearily. "Did a sudden blizzard sweep in during the night and cut off your farm?"

Some of the class tittered at Miss Frost's joke. It was springtime and the snow that had covered the countryside in winter had long since melted.

Mary said nothing. Her head bowed, she concentrated on a spot on the floor, waiting for Miss Frost to continue as we all knew she would.

"Or maybe the rooster forgot to crow this morning to wake you all up?" she went on.

Mary said nothing.

"Please, Miss," said Molly Parker, the school sneak, as she waved her hand in the air for attention. "Please, Miss. Maybe Mary's father drove his tractor into the duckpond and she couldn't get a lift to school."

I glared hard at Molly Parker.

Miss Frost rapped a ruler on her table for the class to quieten down.

"Go to your desk, Mary," she said. "You've caused quite enough commotion for one morning. Let's have no more nonsense from you, young lady."

"I've got a problem," whispered Mary to me as she flopped down into her chair.

"And don't forget," went on Miss Frost, "the school inspector will be here after break, so I want everyone to be on their best behaviour—especially you, Mary. And I want a volunteer to make a nice cup of tea when he arrives. "Polly Crabtree—"she pointed to a girl in the front row— "you can be the volunteer."

"Please, Miss," said Jack Carter, who was mad on cars. "Maybe the inspector's car will be dirty. I volunteer to wash the mud off. That might chuff the old geezer up."

"Very well, Jack," said Miss Frost, once the giggling had stopped. "But perhaps we won't refer to the school inspector as 'the old geezer'. And perhaps someone will volunteer to help you?"

Everyone turned round to Jill Edwards, who was mad on Jack Carter. She shot her hand up. Jack

Carter went red.

"So that's settled," said Miss Frost. "We can get on with some work now that all our little problems are solved."

"My little problem's not solved," whispered Mary. "And it's getting bigger all the time."

At break-time, I found out just what Mary's little problem was. And she was right . . . .

She took me to the cloakroom, to the cupboard in the corner where the janitor stored his brooms and mops and buckets.

And in a cardboard box, I saw—a little lamb!

"It's a pet lamb," said Mary. "It followed me to school, that's why I was late. I sneaked it in here this morning."

"Oh, it's sweet," I said, stroking the wool on its back. Its fleece was white as snow.

"I know," said Mary. "But it's against the rules."

The lamb snuffled at my fingertips.

"I'll sneak it home after school," Mary went on. She sounded ever so worried. "Crumbs. If Miss Frost finds out, she'll have a fit!"

"If Miss Frost finds out what?" said a voice behind us.

We whirled round and saw Molly Parker.

She barged her way between us. Mary tried to close the cupboard door, but—too late.

"Oh," gasped Molly Parker. "You're for it, Mary. I'm going to tell Miss Frost. And the inspector will be there. I'm going to tell Miss Frost as soon as playtime's over!"

With that, she turned on her heel and skipped outside.

In the playground, the other boys and girls played their games, but we didn't feel like joining in.

And then the school inspector drew up in his car. There was mud on the wings and we saw Jack Carter run up with Jill Edwards close on his heels. Polly Crabtree skipped off towards the school kitchen just as the bell went for the end of our break.

Mary and I trudged slowly in. The balloon was about to go up.

The school inspector looked very stern. Jack was right—he was an old geezer.

I looked out of the window and saw Jack struggling with a bucket with one hand, and trying to fight off Jill Edwards with the other, as they went to the tap at the top of the playground.

Then Miss Frost came in, and quick as a flash, Molly Parker shot her hand in the air. She was nearly jumping out of her seat with excitement. Mary was slowly sliding down under her desk.

"Is everyone here?" the school inspector asked Miss Frost, who was looking ever so slightly nervous. She looked around the classroom.

Then, just as her eyes fell on Molly Parker, and as she was about to ask her what she wanted, I jumped up.

"Please, Miss," I blurted. "Please, Miss, everyone's not here. Polly Crabtree's not here. Polly put the kettle on!"

Sniggers ran round the classroom.

Molly Parker tried even harder to get attention.

I looked out of the window.

"And Jack and Jill went up the hill," I said. "To fetch a pail of water!"

Miss Frost looked at me like I was mad. The whole class was rocking with laughter.

"Oh, very well," said Miss Frost with a strange sort of smile playing about her face. "Now let's get on with the lessons, and we'll have no more of this nursery rhyme nonsense."

Molly Parker was nearly standing on top of her desk.

"But, please, Miss," she yelled. "MARY HAD A LITTLE LAMB!"

Let me tell you what happened next . . . .

The class erupted. The school inspector looked as if he was going to choke. Miss Frost slumped down into her chair. When she recovered, she told Molly Parker not to say another word and to stay behind after school.

Which gave Mary and me enough time to sneak the little lamb out of the cupboard and get it safely back to her farm.

Oh—and one other thing. We laughed all the way home.

POND PUZZLE

A man has a pond in the shape of a square. He wants to make it twice as big—but there's a large tree at each corner, and he doesn't want to cut them down. What does he do?

Answer on p. 48

THE KETTLE RHYME

by Ian Serraillier

"My kettle's no use any more," mother said,
Misery you, misery me,
And she hurled the hole-y thing over the hedge.
Misery diddle fa-la!

A robin who found it flew down from a tree:
Merrily you, merrily me,
"This'll do nicely for missus and me."
Merrily diddle fa-la!

When father came home he was angry with mother:
Misery you, misery me,
"I haven't the money to buy us another."
Misery diddle fa-la!

Now robin and family, happily settled,
Merrily you, merrily me,
Peep out—all five—from the hole in the kettle.
Merrily diddle fa-la!

WATCH THE BIRDY!

One of the first signs of spring is when birds start to collect material for their nests—twigs, bits of soft wool, feathers, hair, or whatever each species prefers to make a good place for laying eggs. There are many different kinds of nests and eggs—as many as there are different kinds of bird!

Some to watch out for:

THE SWAN

The male swan (the cob) brings a selection of twigs and other nesting material to the female (the pen). She builds a large, rather untidy nest, and although feathers soon get into it, they aren't used as a lining. As few as three and as many as ten large eggs can be laid. They are pale green.

N.B. *Never* approach a sitting swan. They are big strong birds, and will defend their nests fiercely. They can easily break your arm or leg with a blow from their wing.

THE CUCKOO

Cuckoos are famous—for laying their eggs in other birds' nests! The hen bird makes no nest of her own, but looks for nests made by smaller birds, such as robins, pied wagtails, or hedge sparrows, in which eggs have recently been laid. Often she throws one of these out to make room for her own, bigger, egg. She can lay from six to eighteen eggs like this during one spring season. When the young cuckoo hatches, it throws the other chicks and eggs out of the nest, leaving only one very large and hungry baby for the host parents to feed.

WARNING

- Wild birds are protected by law.
- Never scare a sitting bird off a nest—it will probably desert it, and there will be no baby birds hatched from that nest.
- Never touch an egg in a nest—again, the parents will desert the nest.
- Never damage the plants or structures near a nest.
- If you see a chick which seems to be alone—LEAVE IT! Its parents will feed it when you have gone.

THE SWALLOW

Swallows come back to this country in spring. They spend the winter in warm countries like Africa. The swallow's nest is made of mud and grass, and is moulded on to a wall under the eaves of a house or other building. A swallow may use the same nest several years running. It's lined with soft grass and feathers, and the hen lays up to six long white eggs with red spots. In some places it's considered lucky to have a swallow's nest on your house.

THE PUFFIN

Some birds, like the puffin, nest in burrows! Puffins spend most of their lives at sea, and only come to land during the nesting season. They can dig their own burrows, but they are lazy, and if they can find a rabbit burrow, for example, they will throw out the rabbit by its ears and move in! A female puffin will lay only one egg. It's white with faint speckles—and quickly gets covered with dirt!

THE ROBIN

Often seen in gardens—robins like to build their nests in banks and tree-stumps but have been known to use old tins or empty houses. The nest is made of moss, with dead leaves on the outside, and lined with hair. The hen bird lays from four to six white eggs with pale red spots. Robins can have two or three broods each spring.

THE KESTREL

A bird of prey but often seen in the heart of big cities and along motorways! Kestrels aren't really nest-builders—they may scrape a shallow hollow for their eggs, but prefer to use a high window-ledge or an old crow's or magpie's nest. They lay four to six eggs covered in reddy-brown blotches.

CORKING FUN!

Corks are quite easy to get hold of, and can be made into all kinds of things. How about making some toy animals?

A CROCODILE

You will need:

* 5 or 7 corks of different sizes
* string *or* length of thin wire
* two glass-headed pins
* 4 drawing pins
* paper
* glue
* paints
* helpful grown-up

1 Ask a grown-up to make holes through the corks—a cork-screw will do it, or an awl.
2 Arrange your corks in a row, in descending order of size. Turn the one at the front round, so that the two broadest cork tops are face-to-face. Ask a grown-up to cut a small slit in the end of the smallest cork (see diagram) and also to cut a wedge out of the base of your front cork.
3 Thread your corks together with string or wire. Leave some wire or string between each cork! Bend the wire ends over neatly at each end, or

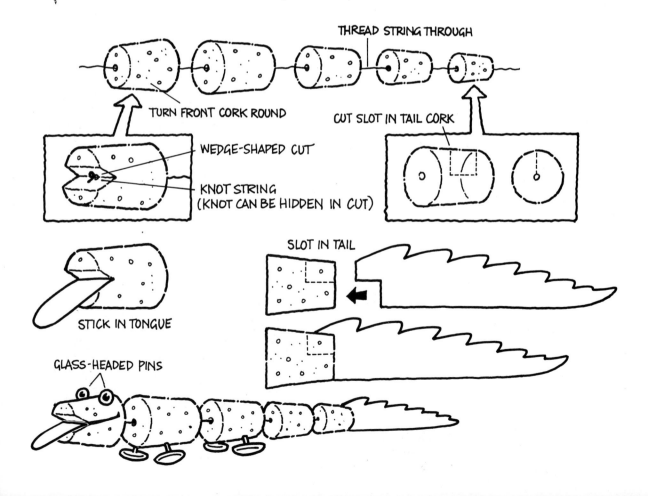

THREAD STRING THROUGH

TURN FRONT CORK ROUND

CUT SLOT IN TAIL CORK

WEDGE-SHAPED CUT

KNOT STRING
(KNOT CAN BE HIDDEN IN CUT)

STICK IN TONGUE

SLOT IN TAIL

GLASS-HEADED PINS

knot the ends of the string, so that the corks don't fall off.

4 Cut a tail-shape out of paper, and paint it green. Slot it into the cut in the smallest cork.

5 Cut a tongue-shape out of paper. Paint it red. When it's dry, glue it into the wedge-shaped cut.

6 Paint your crocodile green all over. Add a crooked grin reaching back from his mouth! Carefully press in the two glass-headed pins for eyes, and the drawing pins for feet.

If you've left gaps between the corks, you'll find that your crocodile will bend about!

A DUCK

You will need:

* a large cork
* paper
* poster paints
* drawing pins
* helpful grown-up

1 Ask your grown-up to cut a slit at each end of the cork (see diagram).

2 Cut the shape of a duck's head and neck, and a duck's tail, out of paper. Paint on the beak, eyes, feathers, etc.

3 When your painted head and tail are quite dry, *carefully* fit them into the slits in the cork. You can add two drawing pins for feet. This will float as it is, if you want your duck for the bath or a pond. If you don't want to sail it, you can paint your duck's body. (The paint would come off in water!)

How about making a whole flock of ducks?

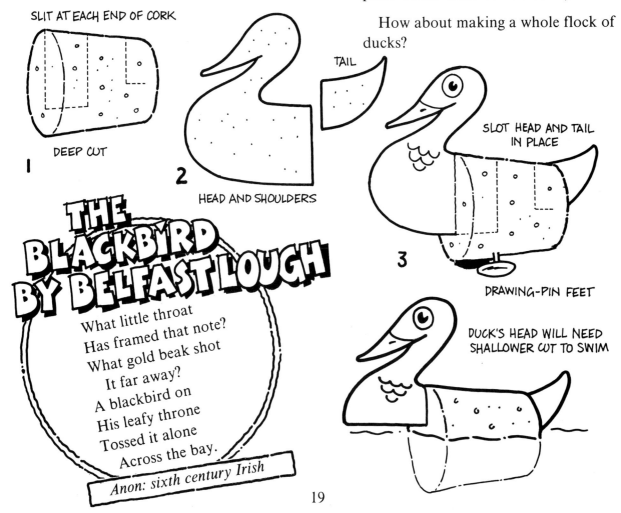

SLIT AT EACH END OF CORK

DEEP CUT

1

TAIL

2

HEAD AND SHOULDERS

SLOT HEAD AND TAIL IN PLACE

3

DRAWING-PIN FEET

DUCK'S HEAD WILL NEED SHALLOWER CUT TO SWIM

THE BLACKBIRD BY BELFAST LOUGH

What little throat
Has framed that note?
What gold beak shot
It far away?
A blackbird on
His leafy throne
Tossed it alone
Across the bay.

Anon: sixth century Irish

MATCH THIS!

Do you ever need to keep small things safe—coins, stamps, buttons, interesting stones, pins or paperclips?

Or can your dolls' house do with a smart chest-of-drawers?

You can make a good container from empty matchboxes.

REMEMBER! Matches are VERY dangerous! You must NEVER play with them!

WHAT YOU WILL NEED...

* six or eight empty matchboxes, all the same size (ask grown-ups to help you collect them)
* paper
* glue
* paints or felt-tips
* very narrow ribbon, or the smallest buttons you can find (shirt cuff buttons are good)

WHAT YOU DO...

1   Glue two matchboxes down the long side, and stick them together. Let them dry.

2   Glue the other matchboxes in pairs. Leave to dry.

3   Coat the tops of one pair of matchboxes with glue, and place the next set *carefully* on it. Let this dry, then repeat the process.

4   When you've finished gluing the block of matchboxes together, cut a strip of paper as wide as the boxes, and long enough to wrap right round the block. With your paints or felt-tips, give this a cheerful pattern. (You could use a strip of wall-paper printed with a small design if you don't feel artistic.)

5   Glue your paper strip right round your matchbox chest-of-drawers. Take care! Make sure the edges of the paper and of the boxes correspond.

6   Take the drawers out of the boxes. *Either* glue on a small loop of narrow ribbon, *or* glue on a button—this will give you a "handle" to use when opening the drawers. *When the glue is dry*, replace the drawers—and you've completed your matchbox chest of drawers!

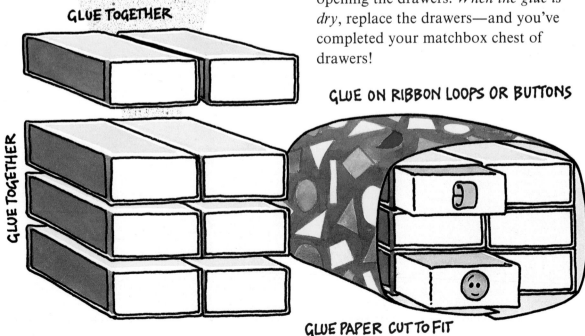

GLUE TOGETHER

GLUE TOGETHER

GLUE ON RIBBON LOOPS OR BUTTONS

GLUE PAPER CUT TO FIT

UPON THE SNAIL
by John Bunyan

She goes but softly, but she goeth sure;
   She stumbles not as stronger creatures do:
Her journey's shorter, so she may endure
   Better than they which do much further go.

She makes no noise, but stilly seizeth on
   The flower or herb appointed for her food,
The which she quietly doth feed upon,
   While others range, and gare,* but find no good.

And though she doth but very softly go,
   Howeyer, 'tis not fast, nor slow, but sure;
And certainly they that do travel so,
   The prize they do aim at, they do procure.

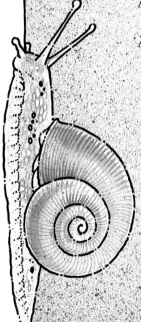

SPRING SAYINGS

April with his beck and bill,
Plants a flower on every hill.

A swarm of bees in May
Is worth a load of hay

In January if sun appear,
March and April will pay full dear.

When apple-trees bloom well in May,
You can eat apples night and day.

March comes in like a lion, and goes out like a lamb.

If it rains on Good Friday and Easter Day,
It's a good year for grass but a poor one for hay.

A dry May and a leaking June
Makes the farmer whistle a merry tune.

RECYCLED EGG-SHELLS

Next time you eat a hard-boiled egg, save the shell. Make a small hole in the bottom with a pin, fill the shell with earth, and plant some cress seeds in it! Keep the seeds watered. Put the shell in an egg-cup while the cress grows— then, when it's sprouted, you can make yourself a lovely egg-and-cress sandwich!

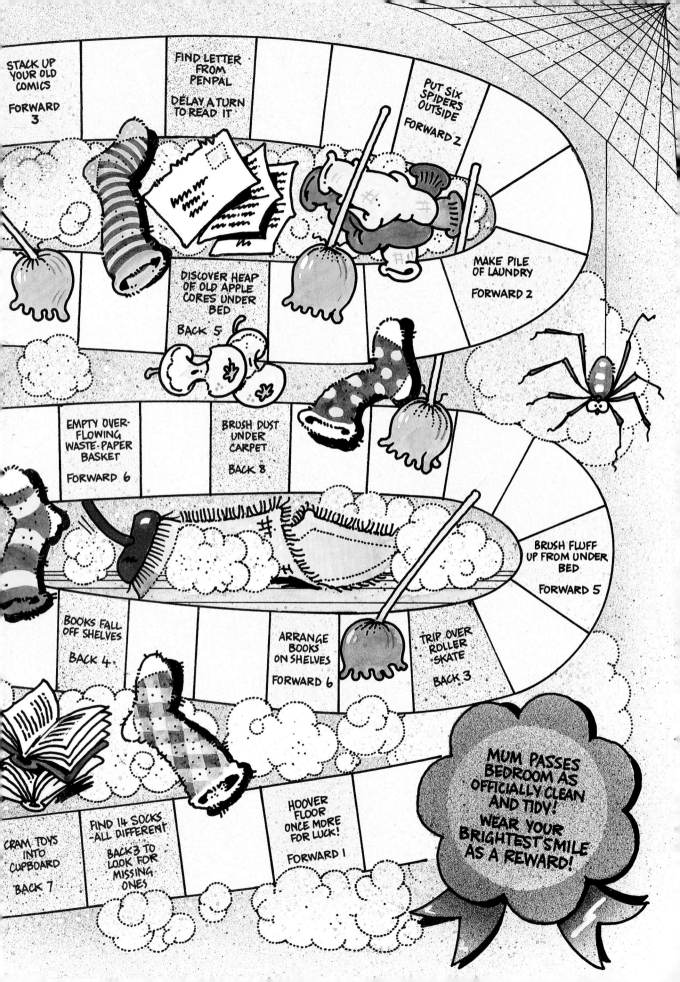

HOW TO HATCH
by ANNE WOODMAN

Some of you will know the square-shaped tangram or seven-board—a square of cardboard cut into triangles, diamonds and a smaller square, which can be used to make most ingenious pictures and patterns. It's an ancient Chinese puzzle!

There's an egg-shaped version, with nine pieces, which is fun to experiment with.

Either: trace the shape of the egg on to thin card, and cut out the pieces marked with *dotted* lines,

or: (if you're good at geometry) make your own egg shape like this—

DRAWING THE EGG

1 Draw a circle of radius 6 cm with centre A.

2 Divide the circle into four quadrants, forming the lines BAC and EAD.

3 Join B to E and E to C, and extend these lines about 5 cm above E.

4 Using centre B, and radius BC, describe an arc until it cuts the extended line BE at G.

5 Using centre C, and radius CB, describe an arc until it cuts the extended line CE at F.

6 With E as the centre, and radius EF, describe an arc to join F and G.

7 Measure this same radius from D along line DA to find point H.

8 With the same radius, and H as the centre, describe an arc to cut line BC at J and K.

9 Extend line AE to cut the arc FG at L.

10 Join H to J and H to K.

11 Cut out the pieces along the *dotted* lines.

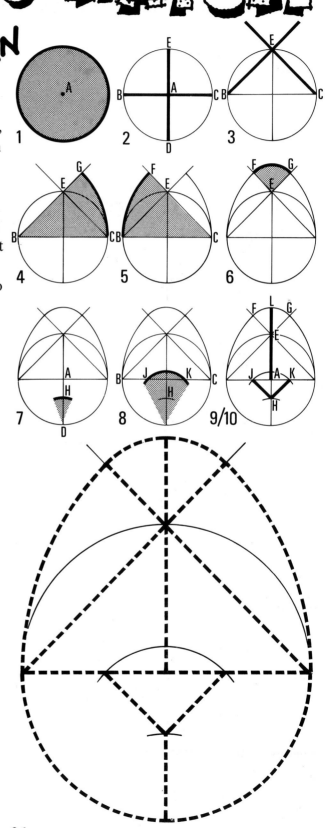

YOUR OWN EGG

Now, can you arrange your pieces into bird shapes? Here are some to get you going!

An egg tangram would make a good present for someone who likes puzzles, or who enjoys patterns and making things.

How about making an egg tangram, decorating the pieces with paints or by covering them with pretty paper, and mounting them in your best bird shape on heavy paper or coloured card, to make a picture or birthday card for somebody special?

THE PRAYER OF THE LITTLE DUCKS

by
CARMEN BERNOLD DE GASTHOLZ

Dear God,
give us a flood of water.
Let it rain tomorrow and always.
Give us plenty of little slugs
and other luscious things to eat.
Protect all folk who quack
and everyone who knows how to swim.

Amen

translated by Rumer Godden

DANCING ROUND

One May Day activity that's still much enjoyed is
dancing round the Maypole. There are many places in
the country where this pretty custom can be seen—
teams of dancers weave intricate patterns with brightly
coloured ribbons round the pole. Barwick-in-Elmet in
Yorkshire has a famous pole, and so does Anstey in
Wiltshire—Anstey's pole is supposed to be the biggest
in the country! It's 96 feet high—that's nearly 30
metres!

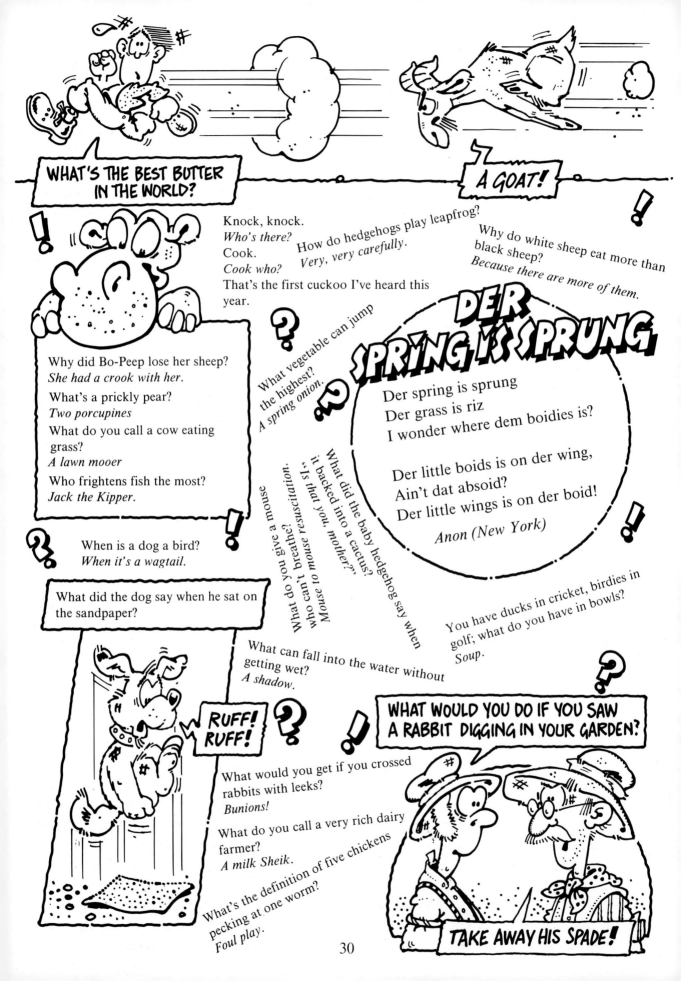

WHAT'S THE BEST BUTTER IN THE WORLD?

A GOAT!

Knock, knock.
Who's there?
Cook.
Cook who?
That's the first cuckoo I've heard this year.

How do hedgehogs play leapfrog?
Very, very carefully.

Why do white sheep eat more than black sheep?
Because there are more of them.

What vegetable can jump the highest?
A spring onion.

Why did Bo-Peep lose her sheep?
She had a crook with her.

What's a prickly pear?
Two porcupines

What do you call a cow eating grass?
A lawn mooer

Who frightens fish the most?
Jack the Kipper.

DER SPRING IS SPRUNG

Der spring is sprung
Der grass is riz
I wonder where dem boidies is?

Der little boids is on der wing,
Ain't dat absoid?
Der little wings is on der boid!

Anon (New York)

What did the baby hedgehog say when it backed into a cactus?
"Is that you, mother?"

What do you give a mouse who can't breathe?
Mouse to mouse resuscitation.

When is a dog a bird?
When it's a wagtail.

What did the dog say when he sat on the sandpaper?

RUFF! RUFF!

What can fall into the water without getting wet?
A shadow.

You have ducks in cricket, birdies in golf; what do you have in bowls?
Soup.

WHAT WOULD YOU DO IF YOU SAW A RABBIT DIGGING IN YOUR GARDEN?

What would you get if you crossed rabbits with leeks?
Bunions!

What do you call a very rich dairy farmer?
A milk Sheik.

What's the definition of five chickens pecking at one worm?
Foul play.

TAKE AWAY HIS SPADE!

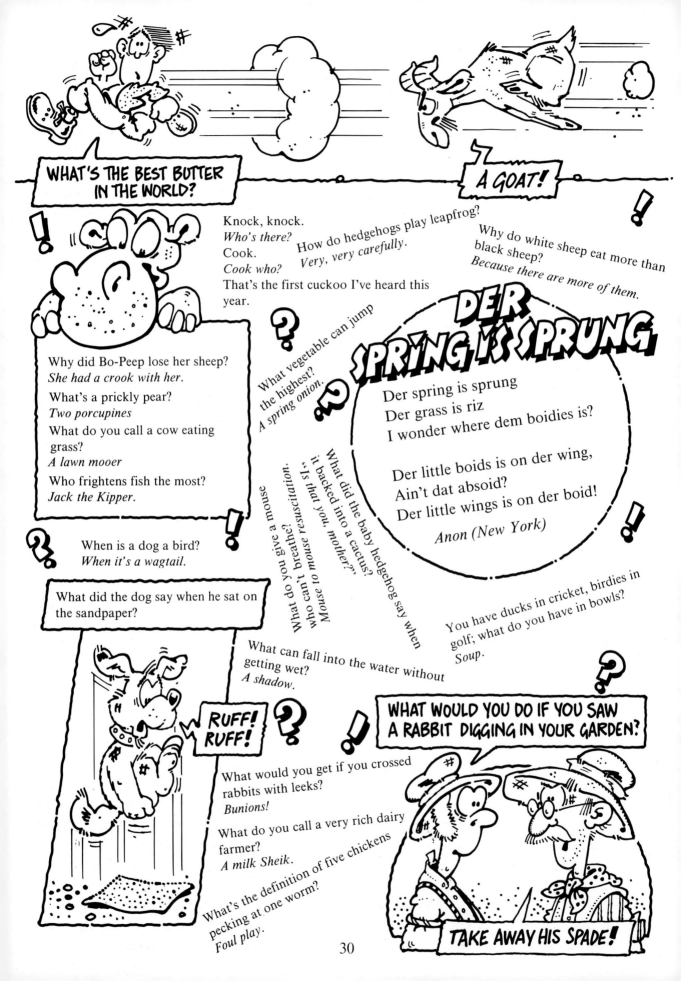

30

HEDGEHOGS & PANCAKES

HEDGIES

Hungry? How about making yourself some hedgehogs to eat?
Here's how—you'll need:

* 450 gms or 1 lb pork sausagemeat *or* finely minced pork
* 1 tsp ground ginger
* ½ tsp each salt and sugar
* 25 gms or 1 oz almond slivers
* a helpful grown-up

1 Ask a grown-up to switch on the oven to 350° (180°C, gas mark 4).
2 Mix the meat and spices together in a bowl.
3 Form the mixture into balls about 5 cms or 2″ in diameter, then pinch out one end to look like a hedgehog's nose.
4 Stick about eight of the almonds into each hedgehog's back, to represent spines.
5 *Carefully* put your hedgehogs on a baking sheet, and cook for half an hour, or until they are nicely browned.

SAUCER PANCAKES

You will need:

* 50 gms or 2 oz softened butter
* 50 gms or 2 oz sugar
* 50 gms or 2 oz flour
* 2 eggs
* 3 dl or ½ pt milk
* jam
* 6 clean old china saucers
* a helpful grown-up.

1 Ask a grown-up to switch the oven on to 425°F (220°C, gas mark 7).
2 Beat the sugar and butter together until it is soft and creamy. (This takes time and muscles!)
3 Add the eggs one at a time, with a teaspoonful of flour for each egg.
4 Add the rest of the flour, using a metal spoon to "fold" it into the mixture.
5 Ask the grown-up to warm the milk slightly. Pour it into the batter, and stir everything together. (If the batter starts to separate out, or curdle, don't worry!)
6 Half-fill your saucers with the mixture.
7 Ask the grown-up to put them in the oven.
8 Bake for 10-15 minutes—then ask the grown-up to take the pancakes out of the oven, and turn them out of the saucers on to some greaseproof paper sprinkled with sugar.
9 Put a spoonful of jam into each pancake, fold in half and allow to cool a little—then eat!

31

CLEAN SHEETS

by Joan Aiken

Once there was a boy called Gus, and his mother said to him, "Gus, it's the day for clean sheets. Take the blankets off your bed, hang them out of the window in the sun, take off the sheets and pillowcases, and turn the mattress. Don't forget to fold the sheets and pillowcases, ready to send to the laundry, but first give them a good shake."

"Why, Ma?" said Gus.

"In case any living creature, a bee or a spider or a fly, has got in among them. We wouldn't want to send a living creature to the laundry."

"That's true," said Gus, hoping very much that he *wouldn't* find a bee or a spider or a cockroach in his bedclothes.

He hung the blankets out of the window to air. Then he took off the top sheet and folded it, ends together, sides together, held the fold under his chin, and folded again into a neat square.

When he took off the bottom sheet and shook it, out fell no living creature but a prickly leaf, blue as a forget-me-not.

"That's a funny-looking leaf," said Gus, and he showed it to his mother.

"What a queer leaf," she said. "I've never seen one like it before. Where can it have come from?"

"Must have blown in the window. I'll show it to my teacher at school," said Gus. "Maybe he will know."

The teacher at school didn't know what kind of a leaf it was either.

"Why not take it to old Mr. Brown at the antique bookshop," he said. "He's read so many books, he might know. Besides, he has a collection of rare plants."

So Gus took the prickly blue leaf to old Mr. Brown, who looked at it through his glasses, and through a lens.

"My boy, you've got a treasure there. What you have is a leaf from the Memory Tree," he said.

"What's the Memory Tree?"

"It grows in the forests of Brazil. Have you had any Brazil nuts lately?"

"We did have some," said Gus.

"A leaf might have got amongst them. The tree was found once, but then it was lost again. Nobody knows where it grows. Just sometimes, once in a way, a leaf turns up."

"What does it do?"

"If you hold it scrunched up in your hand, you can remember anything."

"Anything in the world?"

"Anything in the world."

"Even if it hasn't happened?"

"Even if it never happened."

Gus quickly scrunched up the Memory leaf in his hand. The prickles hurt a little, but not too badly.

"Now, say what you want to remember," said Mr. Brown.

"I want to remember how I was given a zebra for my birthday," said Gus, "and how I rode it right through the town, crossing all the traffic lights

when they were red . . . ."

Right away, that very minute, he could remember his birthday, and how he had looked out of his window to see the zebra standing tied to the front-door knocker. He could remember the zebra's name, Horace, and its red saddle and bridle, with brass bits, and the way all the motorists had hooted when Horace galloped across the lights, and how the police had started after him on their motorbikes, but he had been much too fast for them to catch up.

"My goodness," Gus said to Mr. Brown, "I didn't think memories could be as exciting as that. Now you have a try."

He unclenched his hand. Instantly the Memory leaf unscrumpled and went back to its proper shape. Mr. Brown took it and scrunched it up in *his* hand.

"I want to remember every minute of my first visit to Venice," he said.

"Why don't you remember something that *didn't* happen?" said Gus.

"When you get to my age," said Mr. Brown, "you have plenty of things that you are glad to remember without going to the trouble of inventing."

By the distant smile on his face, it was plain that he was having a very happy time remembering his first visit to Venice.

"Take good care of that leaf, my boy," he said. "You've got a treasure there and you're never likely to find another."

Gus took the leaf home and told his father and mother what it was.

"Fancy!" said his mother. "Just let me have it a moment so I can remember where I hid the key to my desk that time when we went to visit Aunt Alice five years ago."

She scrumpled up the leaf in her hand. Instantly she remembered that she had buried the key in a pot of geraniums. Unluckily the geraniums had died long ago and the pot of earth had been thrown away. But Gus's mother also remembered Cousin Flora's address in Minnesota, and the title of a book she had read about in a magazine and wanted to get from the library, and a recipe for chutney Mrs. Swale had given her that she had forgotten to write down, and several things she had meant to tell the doctor about her rheumatism when she saw him the day before.

"Here, let me have a go," said Gus's father. And he scrunched up the leaf in his hand and remembered the name of the boy who had sat next to him in his first year at school, and a very good football match between Arsenal and Tottenham in 1948, and the taste of the date shortbreads that his grandmother used to make.

"Now it's my turn!" said Gus. "After all, I found the leaf."

"It's your bedtime," said his mother.

So Gus had to go to bed, but he took the leaf with him. And lying in bed, holding the leaf scrunched up in his hand, he remembered floating down the Colorado river in a canoe past great golden cliffs. He remembered flying across the Gobi desert on the back of an eagle. He remembered winning the Derby on the Queen's horse. He remembered getting ten out of ten for sums every day for a whole term. He remembered the sarcastic thing he had said to Mr. Formby the history teacher. He remembered finding a sword stuck in a rock and pulling it out. He remembered scoring the winning goal in an ice-hockey match. He remembered getting into the pilot's seat of a small aeroplane he had been given. Then he went to sleep . . .

Next day he found the Memory leaf where it had slipped down to the bottom of the bed, and took it to school. He showed it to his best friend, Andrew, who had a go at using it, and remembered that a boy called Ted Stone owed him two packets of chewing-gum.

"That's a boring sort of thing to remember," said Gus.

Ted, when reminded about the gum, had a go at the leaf, and remembered eating all the doughnuts in the world without being sick.

"Tell you what," said Andrew, "why don't you take it to the Queen?"

"Why?" said Gus. "What's the point? I'd rather keep it myself."

"Don't be stupid. Take it to the Queen, get her to hold it, and remind her how you found her crown when it was lost. Then you'll get the reward."

The Queen of that country was always losing her crown; generally it turned up quite soon, hanging on a lamp-post, or among the cabbages in a supermarket, or on a seat in the park or a hatstand in a cafe, wherever she had happened to take it off.

Sometimes it didn't turn up, and then she had a new one made.

"But I never have found her crown," said Gus.

"No, but she'll remember if you tell her so."

Gus wasn't interested in the reward, but he was quite pleased at a chance to see the Queen. So he went along to the palace on Saturday morning, at which time the Queen was always at home to any of her subjects who wanted to drop in and consult her.

"Good morning your Majesty," said Gus, when he had brushed his hair and

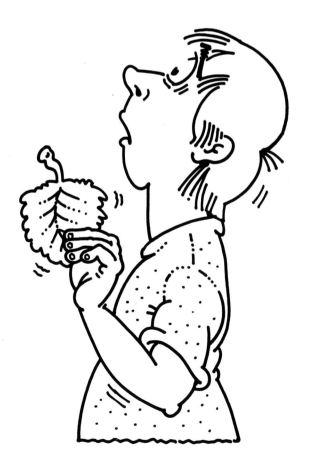

put on a clean jersey and passed all the guards and done the best bow he could.

"Good morning. What can I do for you?" said the Queen.

"I've brought this rare leaf for you to look at," said Gus. "Hold it scrunched up in your hand, your Majesty, and you'll be able to remember how I found your crown last time you lost it."

The Queen scrunched up the Memory leaf in her hand.

Then she frowned at Gus.

"Yes!" she said. "I can remember that you found my crown. I can also remember that you stuck it on your head and galloped right through the town on a zebra, passing all the traffic lights at red and causing unheard-of traffic chaos. What is more, when you *did* bring the crown back, it was badly dented, and several of the diamonds had fallen out."

"I-I'm sorry, Ma'am," stammered Gus, very much taken aback. "I d-don't remember that myself."

"In fact the fines that you owe for dangerous zebramanship exactly equal the amount the reward would have been," said the Queen soberly, giving him back the leaf, "and you are lucky I don't send you to prison for damaging royal property."

What she said made Gus so nervous that he dropped the leaf on to the marble floor.

A draught blew it clean out of the palace window, across the main square of the town, over the river, and far away, who knows where.

Gus never found a Memory leaf again.

Perhaps it was just as well.

SPRING SPORTS SPECTACULAR

One of the toughest steeplechases in the world is the Grand National. Since 1839 it's been run at Aintree, near Liverpool. The course is $4\frac{1}{2}$ miles long, (that's over seven kilometres,) and there are 30 jumps—Becher's Brook is so difficult that the name is used outside racing to denote a real hazard. The Grand National is run just before Easter each year.

Dark blue or light blue? Even people who have no connections with Oxford or Cambridge Universities take sides for the annual Boat Race, rowed over a $4\frac{1}{2}$ mile (over seven kilometres) stretch of the river Thames from Putney to Mortlake. The race dates from 1829, and is the longest important boat race in the world. The race is fixed for a Saturday before Easter. The exact Saturday changes from year to year, depending on the tides in the River Thames.

The most famous car race in America is the Indianapolis 500. It's run on Memorial Day, a public holiday at the end of May, and the course is 500 miles (over 800 kilometres) round a circuit of $2\frac{1}{2}$ miles (that's about 4 kilometres). Only the 33 fastest cars from the four-lap qualification races take part.

The Last Great Race in the world is held every March—in Alaska! It's the toughest race in the world, and commemorates the time in 1925 when an outbreak of diphtheria struck the town of Nome. The only way to get the doctors the serum they needed to fight the disease was for men to take it on sledges pulled by teams of dogs. They used an old road called the Iditarod Trail. Nowadays, dog-sledge teams race across more than 1600 kilometres (almost 1,000 miles) of savage country from Anchorage to Nome. The Iditarod race is so difficult there's even a prize for coming in last!

BUTTERFLY SURPRISE

Treat someone in your family, or a friend, to a Butterfly Surprise. Or you can even make this for yourself—and brighten up your room!

You will need:
* wooden "dolly" shaped clothes pegs
* glue
* paper
* paint
* scissors

1 Fold the paper in half, and draw the shape of butterflies' wings on one side. Cut round the outline, so that you end up with a complete pair of wings.
2 You can either paint them like a real butterfly, or make up your own colourful design. Remember! Paint one side of the paper first, and *let it dry completely* before turning it over and painting the other side.
3 Now put a thin line of glue down the fold in the paper, and stick it to the clothes peg. When it's dry, you can either paint a face on the top of the peg or, if you're very clever with your hands, you can stick a narrow strip of paper painted black and bent in two on to the top, to represent antennae.

This makes a most unusual birthday card, or you can decorate tables with your butterflies. How about a colourful row on the washing line? The pegs make a useful present, too.

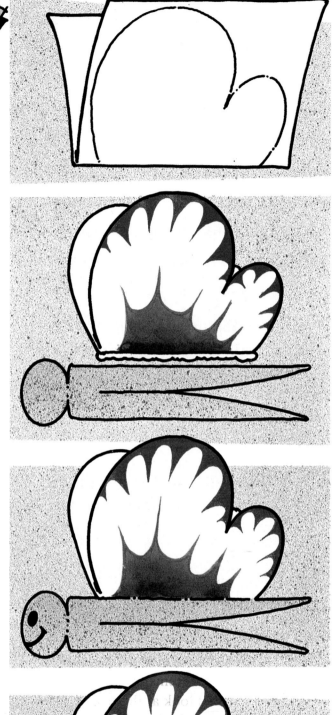

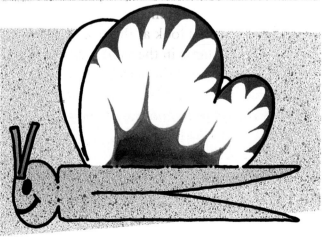

SEA AND SKY

BEAR, LION AND A QUEEN

It's very satisfying to be able to identify groups of stars, or constellations, and you can impress your friends, too! There are some good constellations to spot in the spring sky. Look out, if you can, about 9.00 at night in April, and see if you can find these:

☆ THE PLOUGH

This is a famous group of stars, and quite easy to spot. At this time of year, it's almost overhead. Look at it carefully, for it will be useful as a sign-post to other constellations.

   The stars of the Plough are part of a bigger group, known as The Great Bear (Ursa Major) or King Charles's Wain, or in America, the Big Dipper.

☆ POLARIS

From the Plough, you can find Polaris, the Pole Star. It's important, because the axis of the earth's rotation points at it, and it never seems to move. So whenever you look at the sky at night, the Pole Star is in the same place! The Pole Star is 600 times as bright as the sun, but it's 250 light years away, so doesn't look exceptionally bright. Draw a mental line from Merak through Dubhe, and on out, and you'll come to Polaris, in the constellation Ursa Minor, or the Little Bear. It's the bear's tail!

☆ CASSIOPEIA

Now go back to the Plough. This time we're looking for Cassiopeia, (say "Cass-ee-oh-pay-ah") who was the Queen in the Greek story of Perseus. Her stars make a shape like a "W" or an "M" in the sky. Draw your imaginary line from Mizar in the Plough through Polaris, and on out, and you'll find her. She never sets in England, and you'll see the Milky Way running through her, too.

☆ THE LION

Use the stars of the Plough, too, to find Leo, the Lion, in the south of the night sky.

   This time you want Megrez and Phad—a gently curving line through them and heading south will reach Leo. One end of the constellation is a sickle shape, which looks like a question mark written backwards.

☆ ORION

One famous constellation that everyone ought to know is Orion, the Huntsman. Orion sets in the summer, but his familiar shape can still be seen in early spring if you look towards the west.

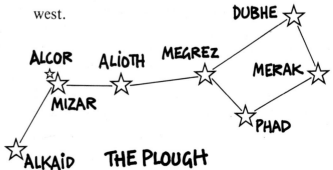

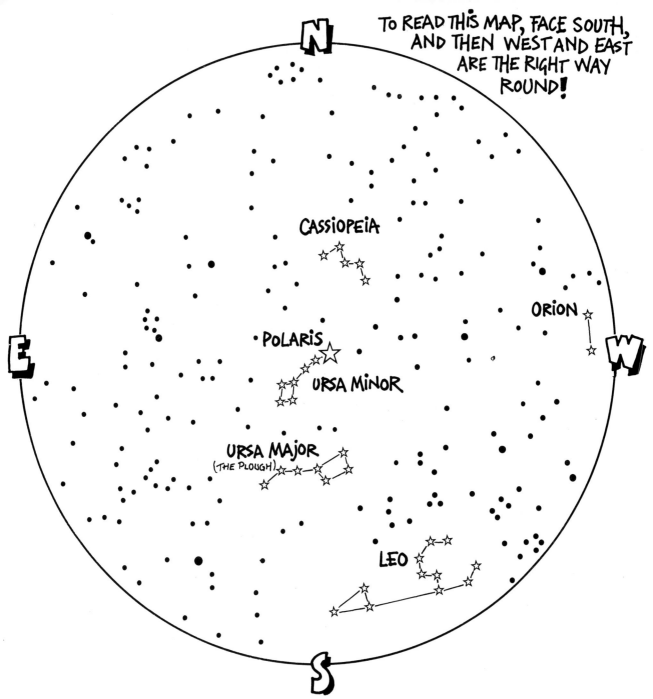

N

CASSIOPEIA

ORION

•POLARIS

URSA MINOR

URSA MAJOR
(THE PLOUGH)

LEO

E

W

S

Gravity is the force that causes things to fall down and hit the ground, and which keeps us sticking on to the Earth! The moon's gravity is weak, but it does have some force. The sun also exerts a gravitational pull.

Although the moon's gravity isn't strong, it influences our planet, by pulling at the water in the seas. As the earth and the moon spin round in the sky, the water rises and falls, in what we call "tides".

The earth and the moon are also circling the sun. In spring (and in autumn too) the earth, the moon and the sun are in a more-or-less straight line. This means that the water in the sea is pulled both by the moon *and* the sun—with the result that tides rise and fall dramatically! These very high tides are called Spring Tides.

Fat Tuesday and Farewell Flesh

For centuries the Christian church has kept the six weeks before Easter as a special time in which people gave up eating meat and other rich food, and studied and thought about the meaning of Good Friday and Easter. Lent starts on Ash Wednesday, so the Tuesday before, known in this country as Shrove Tuesday, is a good day to finish up the forbidden foods, and to have a last party before becoming serious!

In France, Mardi Gras (Fat Tuesday) is the day for great celebrations. Mardi Gras in Nice is the most famous—but now the festivities have stretched, and Mardi Gras starts about three weeks before the Tuesday itself! There are huge parades through the streets, presided over by the King of the Oceans and the Seas; there are bands, people walking about in all kinds of fantastic costumes, sacks of confetti—and each Wednesday a Battle of Flowers, in which everyone throws irises, lilies, mimosas, carnations and other blossoms!

France used to rule part of the south-western United States, and Mardi Gras is celebrated there, too. The biggest and most famous festival is held in New Orleans in the state of Louisiana.

A third city renowned for Mardi Gras fun is Rio de Janiero in Brazil. Like Nice and New Orleans the festivities start weeks before Fat Tuesday itself, and the streets are full of colour and music as happy and wonderfully dressed people join in the fun!

Venice in Italy also celebrates the Tuesday before Lent—with a Carnival. This name comes from Latin, and means "Farewell Flesh". Great masked balls are held in the ancient palaces, and the guests, wearing marvellous fancy dresses covered with silk cloaks called "dominoes" and disguised by masks, float along the canals in gondolas on their way to the parties.

SOME OTHER FESTIVALS AROUND THE WORLD

Holi is celebrated in March by Indian communities. It's a festival of fun—people play tricks on each other, a bit like April Fool's Day. In some places young men roam the streets, and pelt anyone they see with paint and dyes, so you don't go out unless you want to end up looking like a mobile patchwork quilt.

The Chinese New Year falls in spring, and is the occasion for enormous merrymaking. The Chinese group their years into series of twelve, each named after an animal. They are the Rat, the Buffalo, the Tiger, the Cat, the Dragon, the Snake, the Horse, the Goat, the Monkey, the Rooster, the Dog and the Pig. Each animal represents certain characteristics and virtues, which should influence the year. The date of New Year depends on the moon, and doesn't fall on the same day of each Western year. When the day comes, there is feasting and firecrackers—and huge, coloured dragons, symbols of good luck, are made and paraded through the streets.

In Japan, Girls' Day and Boys' Day are both celebrated in spring. Girls' Day is 3rd March. During the day, girls go to each other's houses to look at and admire the splendid collections of dolls which are on display. Boys' Day is 5th May—the end of Golden Week, during which there are five holidays! On Boys' Day families put up poles in their gardens, and from these fly paper streamers shaped like carp—these fish symbolise energy and determination. Inside their houses, people display miniature soldiers and horses, which, like the dolls, are much admired.

HOME-THOUGHTS, FROM ABROAD
by Robert Browning

O to be in England
Now that April's there,
And whoever wakes in England
Sees, some morning, unaware,
That the lowest boughs and the brushwood sheaf
Round the elm-tree bole are in tiny leaf,
While the chaffinch sings on the orchard bough
In England—now!

And after April, when May follows,
And the whitethroat builds, and all the swallows!
Hark, where my blossom'd pear-tree in the hedge
Leans to the field and scatters on the clover
Blossoms and dewdrops—at the bent spray's edge—
That's the wise thrush; he sings each song twice over,
Lest you should think he never could recapture
The first fine careless rapture!
And though the fields look rough with hoary dew,
All will be gay when noontide wakes anew
The buttercups, the little children's dower
—Far brighter than this gaudy melon-flower!

FROGGY FROLICS

When do frogs think in water?
When they ponder.

What goes "Croak! Croak!" when it is misty?
A frog-horn.

Where do frogs hang their coats?
In a croakroom.

What would you get if you crossed a set of bagpipes with a frog?
Hopscotch.

DID YOU KNOW—that on 12th June 1954, frog rain fell in Birmingham? Thousands of small frogs cascaded down in the rain, landing on umbrellas and hopping about in the roads.

Where do tadpoles that lose their tails go?

To a retail shop.

Where do frogs keep their savings?

What happened to the frog when it died?
The poor thing simply croaked.

THE FROG
ANON. (FRENCH CANADIAN)

What a wonderful bird the frog are—
When he stand he sit almost;
When he hop, he fly almost.
He ain't got no sense hardly;
He ain't got no tail hardly either.
When he sit, he sit on what he ain't got almost.

In the river bank.

What's white outside, green inside, and hops?   *A frog sandwich.*

A KITCHEN GARDEN

Spring is the time for growing things, and people with gardens are usually hard at work on their fruit, vegetables, and flowers. But don't worry if you have no garden! There are plenty of things you can grow, no farther away than the kitchen.

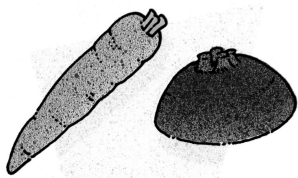

CARROTS AND BEETROOTS

If you have any of these *fresh* vegetables in the kitchen, and there are the stubs of the old leaf stalks still showing at the top, you're in business! (Don't try growing cooked or frozen vegetables—it won't work!)

Punch holes in the bottom of an empty yogurt or margarine pot (or use a proper flower pot, if you can get one). Fill your pot with soil-less compost, well dampened.

Cut a generous 2 or 3 centimetres (about an inch) from the top of your root, and plant in the pot with the top of the root level with the soil. Keep well watered, and you should soon see leaves sprouting. The carrot has delicate green ferns, and the beetroot distinctive purpley-green leaves. If anyone in your family likes arranging flowers, they'll want to use some of your leaves!

Beware of the Beetroot! Cut beetroot "bleeds"—and the red juice stains very badly. So take care it doesn't get on you or on anything else. Keep some old newspaper under your beetroot and pot while you plant it, in case of accidents. Wipe any work surface immediately!

PINEAPPLES

You can do the same thing with a pineapple top! Leave your cut section of fruit on its side for two days to dry out before you plant it.

Then, when you've got it in its pot, enclose the whole thing in a clear polythene or plastic bag, and keep it in the warmest, lightest place you can find.

The pineapple is a tropical plant, and the bag is to try and convince it that it's in a nice warm climate, not a cold one. You can take the bag off when you see new leaves forming—but still keep your plant warm and in the light.

APPLES, ORANGES AND LEMONS

Seeds from oranges and lemons, and from *ripe* apples, can be planted—put four or five in each pot, and water them carefully. Use the polythene bag trick to keep them warm and draught-free. Put the pot on a warm window-sill, too. When shoots show two leaves each, very carefully put each one in its own small pot. Keep well-watered and out of full sun. Tangerines grow faster than oranges, and you are more likely to get edible fruit in the end—but you'll be very lucky if you do! All citrus plants have very sweetly-scented flowers, which are lovely even without fruit.

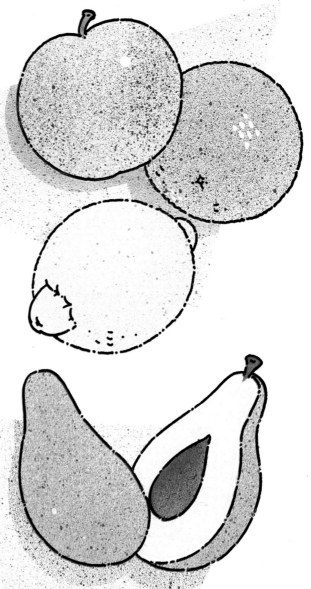

AVOCADOES

Many people try to grow plants from avocado stones, and are disappointed. There's always the risk that a particular stone is not fertile, but you can give yourself a fighting chance of success!

Take a stone from a ripe avocado, and soak it in *warm* water for two days—lukewarm water can be kept tepid by being left on a radiator or put in the airing cupboard. (Ask if you can do this, otherwise there could be trouble!)

Now take an ordinary glass jam jar, and fill it up with lukewarm water. Suspend your avocado stone in the water so that the base (the broad end with the wrinkled skin) is just touching the water. You can use toothpicks, or cocktail sticks, or straightened-out hairpins, pushed a little way into the stone, to hold it in the right position. Place your jam jar in a darkish warm corner (ask about the airing cupboard again), and keep it topped up with warm water.

It can take as much as four weeks for the roots to show, so be patient. If the water goes cloudy and starts to smell, or if after a month nothing has happened, try again with another stone. When you've got a lot of roots, transfer your avocado to a largish pot of compost (about 15 cms, or 6″ across, if you can manage it). Keep the plant well-watered. When the leaf stalk is about 15 cms tall, nip out the top. This will encourage side branches, and you'll get a nice bushy plant, instead of a tall straggly one.

THE PEOPLE UPSTAIRS
by Ogden Nash

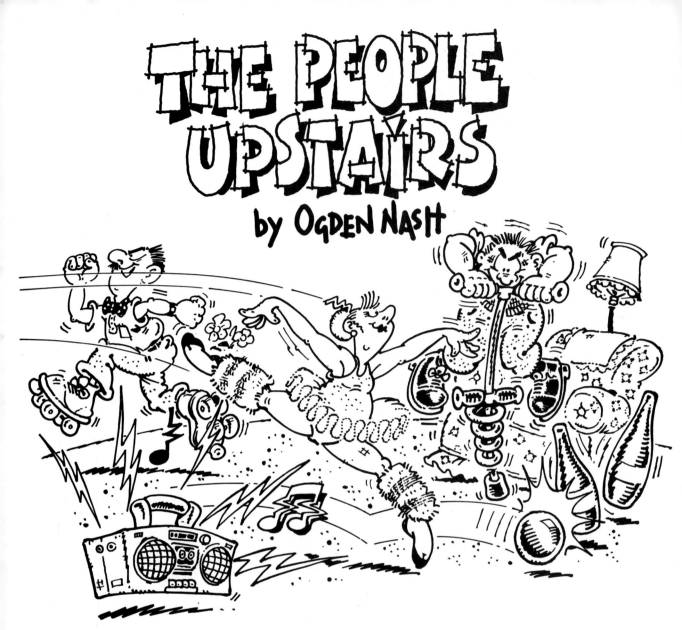

The people upstairs all practice ballet.
Their living room is a bowling alley.
Their bedroom is full of conducted tours.
Their radio is louder than yours.
They celebrate week-ends all the week.
When they take a shower, your ceilings leak.
They try to get their parties to mix
By supplying their guests with Pogo sticks,
And when their orgy at last abates,
They go to the bathroom on roller skates.
I might love the people upstairs wondrous
If instead of above us, they just lived under us.

POSTCARD PUZZLE

On one of those wet days that happen even in the best of springs, why not challenge your friends to walk through a postcard!

When they can't do it, show them how.

Take an ordinary postcard, and cut it across the middle. (fig A)

Take care not to cut right to the edge—you'll need to leave about 1 cm uncut at top and bottom.

Next, make at least seven cuts down each side towards the central cut. Don't let any of these reach the middle. (fig. B)

Now cut across the central line between the outside cuts. Don't let these reach the outside edge of the postcard. (fig C)

Now your postcard will open up into a ring—big enough for you to walk through!

Button to chin till May be in;
Cast not a clout till May be out.

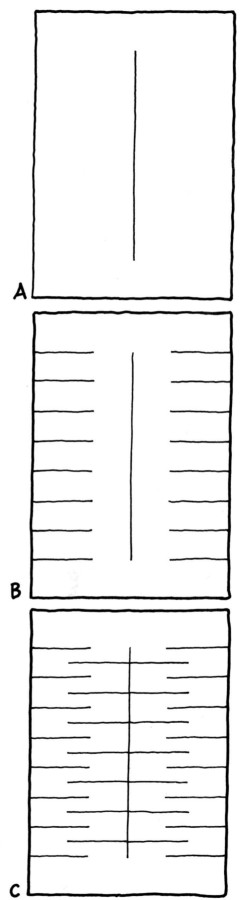

A

B

C

FOUR DUCKS ON A POND

by William Allingham

Four ducks on a pond,
A grass-bank beyond,
A blue sky of spring,
White clouds on the wing;
What a little thing
To remember for years—
To remember with tears!

POND PUZZLE ANSWER:

The man made his pond twice as big
like this:

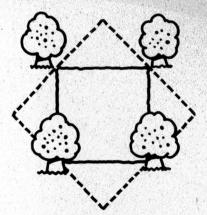